THE CHP BOOK OF

AMAZING RESCUES

Editors:
Janet Stewart, B.A., M.A.
Nadia Pelowich

Art Director:
Rick Rowden

CHP BOOKS

Hayes Publishing Ltd., 3312 Mainway, Burlington, Ontario L7M 1A7, Canada
2045 Niagara Falls Blvd., Unit 14, Niagara Falls, NY 14304, U.S.A.

PRINTED IN HONG KONG

Copyright © 1987 by Hayes Publishing Ltd.

ISBN 0-88625-151-6

CONTENTS

4

SHIPWRECKED IN ALASKA

Written by Janet Stewart
Illustrated by Eugene Pawczuk and Rick Rowden

Twelve-year-old Jena and her older brother and sister, Randy and Cindy, lived with their father on a sailboat they had built together, called *Home*. Since their father suffered from a rheumatic illness and couldn't work at a regular job, the family lived on the boat, and the children received their schooling from correspondence courses. Every six weeks or so, Elmo would sail the *Home* from Suemez Island in Alaska to Prince Rupert, Canada, where the three children had dental work done. So when they cast off from Prince Rupert on February 13, 1979, on their voyage home, things seemed the way they'd always been. The weather was good, and no storms were forecast for the area.

Later that evening, the wind picked up and snow started piling up on the windows of the pilothouse. Big, breaking waves and poor visibility made Elmo drop the sea anchor as he tried to stop the *Home*'s journey across Dixon Entrance. If they entered the strait in this storm, they were doomed! The boat continued to move, so Elmo got fifteen-year-old Randy to drop the headsail and use it to form a bag, like a parachute, behind the boat. This acted like another anchor to slow the drift of the *Home* into the dangerous strait. The seas continued to grow more violent and the storm worsened. Weak and exhausted from seasickness, the four of them lay in their bunks trying to overcome their fear. What had begun as an ordinary day was quickly turning into a frightening nightmare!

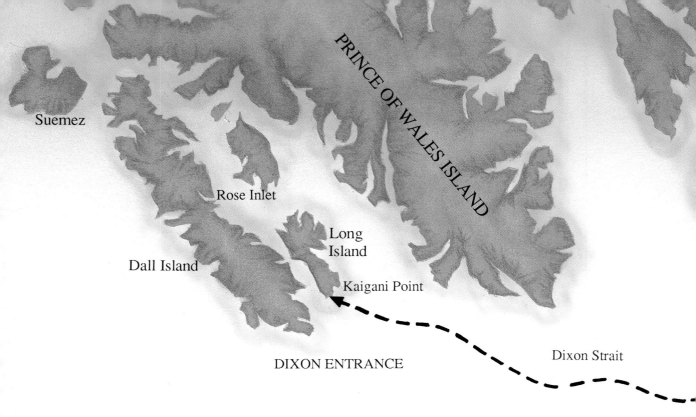

Suemez

Rose Inlet

PRINCE OF WALES ISLAND

Long
Island

Dall Island

Kaigani Point

DIXON ENTRANCE

Dixon Strait

The *Home* had no radio or CB, and Elmo had forgotten to check in and out with customs at Prince Rupert, so no one knew they were out in the storm. After 24 hours, with the seas growing more and more violent, Elmo knew they couldn't survive for long.

Sometime near midnight the next night, Cindy saw a dark object through the snow. She knew it was land, but how close were they? If they were too close, the strength of the waves could push them into the cliffs and they would all die. When she told her father, he jumped up in terror and looked out into the night. A short distance away water exploded against rocky cliffs. As the boat was pushed closer to the cliffs, Elmo realized the only way they could escape injury was to head south, where there were fewer rocks.

Using the rudder that had been broken earlier by a pounding wave, Elmo tried to turn the boat. With only 45 meters (50 yards) to go, the sea line caught in the propeller and the engine died. Now it seemed nothing could stop the raging waves from pushing the *Home* into the rocks. Elmo came face to face with the

truth: If they wanted to get out alive, they would have to try and swim through the icy water! Now he had to tell the kids. Knowing there wasn't much time left, he turned to Jena, Cindy and Randy: "We've got about ten minutes left."

Their hearts pumping in fear, Jena, Cindy and Randy quickly stuffed articles they might need into plastic bags and put them in the Sport-Yak (their plastic skiff), hoping it would reach shore. Bundled in their 'floatcoats' (special winter jackets designed for warmth and water resistance), Jena, Cindy, Randy and their father jumped overboard where the water's icy temperature took their breath away and pulled at their clothing. All of them were pushed separately toward the rocks by the current. Cold and battered, each spent the night alone, unsure if the others had made it.

The next morning, numb with cold, the four of them reunited and started a fire using matches from a glass jar Randy had put in his jacket, and wood they found scattered about on shore. Barefoot, they searched the beach and found some foam pads, a sail from their boat, a fuel tank with some diesel fuel in it, makeshift

A L A S K A

BRITISH
COLUMBIA

Course of the *Home*

CANADA

Prince
Rupert

shoes, and a few other useful articles. They used the sail to make a shelter over two large rocks, and the foam pads were squeezed out and placed over and underneath them to provide protection from the cold. Digging up some mussels, they cooked them over the fire. This was the first thing they had eaten in over 36 hours. Throughout the night they stayed under the shelter and tended the fire. Wet clothes and below-freezing temperatures made sleeping impossible.

At daybreak, on February 16, the family realized they were stranded near the southern tip of Long Island, Alaska. Called Kaigani Point, this area was deserted, and if the Wortmans were going to survive, they would have to leave. It had been three days since the family left Prince Rupert.

Luckily, Elmo was familiar with the area and knew that at the north end of Long Island, across the channel, was Dall Island and an occupied cabin. This was their only hope! The best way to get there was to build a raft and try to paddle up the west side of Long Island, about 45 km (25 miles). The four of them tried to stuff pieces of styrofoam through the cracks in the bottom of the Sport-Yak, and although the water could still get in, the foam provided enough buoyancy so the boat would float.

The next day, Randy and Jena took the Sport-Yak and went by sea to an inlet further north. Cindy and Elmo walked overland to join them in a cove area, sheltered from the wind and littered with firewood. This was the fourth day since the shipwreck without any real food. The kids were getting very tired and couldn't do much without feeling dizzy and sick.

7

Finally, by February 18, they got a raft built by putting two logs on either side of the Sport-Yak and tying them together. The raft floated and they were off! After a day of drifting and rowing, the tired crew pulled into a sheltered cove. Curled up under the sail, they had their first real sleep in days.

On February 19, they cast off again and made it to within a day's traveling of Rose Inlet, the cabin and their safety. However, another storm prevented them from continuing and kept them camped for four days. On the 24th, Randy told his father the girls were very weak, and unless something was done, they wouldn't last much longer. So, Randy and Elmo decided to go on alone, planning to return for the girls in about three hours.

When they were within view of the cabin, they reached a standstill! All around the shoreline for several meters was saltwater ice - too thick to paddle through and too soft to walk on. They abandoned the raft close to shore and struggled through water and deep snow to the cabin. The door was unlocked. Randy and his father went inside, and Randy headed straight for the kitchen, and food! It had been eleven days since Randy had eaten food other than clams and mussels. Elmo started a fire in the wood stove and they sat close to it, eating and warming themselves. Their frozen feet started to thaw with the warmth from the fire, and the pain was terrible.

Elmo tried to use the CB in the cabin to contact help, but it wouldn't work. They tried to flash an SOS to any boats in the area, but no help came. Elmo and Randy lay down and tried to overcome their pain, from both their frozen feet and the sadness they felt for Jena and Cindy, lying freezing in the snow. Desperately wanting to help the girls, but crippled by frostbitten feet, they lay for nine days, soaking them to bring down the swelling. The pain was so great they couldn't walk. Feeling helpless, they sat and thought about the girls alone on the beach. Elmo was sure that after all this time they must be dead!

The next day, they left the cabin with the aid of crutches made from old sticks. They found a fiberglass boat near the dock, buried under snow. They patched it up and decided to go back and get the girls' bodies.

Setting out on March 10, Randy paddled while Elmo bailed water out of the leaking boat. Both feared what they were going to find at Keg Point. It had been 25 days since the shipwreck, and the girls had been alone on the beach for fourteen of them.

When they arrived at Keg Point, Elmo walked slowly up the beach while Randy hung back. Elmo called out the girls' names. He waited in dread. Then he heard a noise. Taking off the sail that covered Cindy and Jena, Elmo saw that they were both alive. Tears of joy ran down his face as he hugged and kissed them. They looked like skeletons, but they were alive, and that was all that mattered! They had survived by laying still, sucking on snow and seaweed and talking to each other. Neither of them could walk, so Randy and Elmo carried them to the boat. They headed back to Rose Inlet, the girls eating all the peanut butter sandwiches and popcorn Randy had brought.

On the return trip to the cabin, they heard motors and saw two trollers. They tried to yell and wave to attract attention, but no one heard or saw them. Once they got to the cabin, they carried the girls up, washed their sore bodies and fed them. Someone had been at the cabin while Randy and Elmo were gone. They hoped whoever it was had gone for help. Then, on March 11, they heard the buzz of a helicopter. It was the big, old slow chopper the Alaska coast guard used for rescue missions. They could scarcely believe it! They were saved!

The coast guard took them to a Ketchikan hospital, where Randy, Cindy and Elmo had operations on their feet. After short stays in the hospital, they all went home. Their lives returned to normal, and while the pain of the experience faded, the memory would be there forever, reminding them how they had survived what most people can't even imagine.

APOLLO 13 TO MISSION CONTROL...

"We've got a problem here."

Written by Janet Stewart
Illustrated by Gary Wein

Captain James A. Lovell Jr., Fred W. Haise Jr., and John L. Swigert Jr. were on board the Apollo 13 spacecraft, preparing for America's third lunar landing. At 2:15 p.m., April 11, 1970, they launched their spaceship for the moon.

Two days later, the crew reported a loud bang, followed by a sharp drop in pressure in one of the two liquid oxygen tanks in the service module section of the spaceship. Gases flowed into space and the craft started to roll. Remaining calm, John Swigert radioed Mission Control. His message: "Hey, we've got a problem here."

Hanging over 320,000 km (200,000 miles) away in space, the lives of the three astronauts were dependent on the experts at Mission Control. Flight controllers, spacecraft engineers and space agency officials began to formulate plans that would bring the crippled ship back to earth and save the lives of the three astronauts. Their life-and-death decisions were heavily based on data from a bank of five computers.

Using millions of bits of information from space, fed into the computers by equipment on board the Apollo 13, decisions were made on rescue plans for the crew. Four reasonable options were considered: The 'free-return trajectory,' the 'super-fast return,' the 'Atlantic Ocean splashdown,' and the 'Pacific Ocean splashdown.'

Further research showed that the first three plans had flaws and were rejected. Finally, after more than twelve hours agonizing over the data, flight director Glynn S. Lunney, along with aeronautical engineers Gerald Griffen, Eugene Kranz and Milton Windler, and dozens of flight controllers and experts, chose the fourth rescue plan.

Under this plan, the astronauts would keep the lunar module part of the spacecraft attached to the command module. Called Aquarius, this two-man lunar landing craft would serve as a lifeboat for the three men. They would have to remain in the Aquarius for the trip home, leaving only for short rests in the larger command module. Their lifeboat, built to accommodate two men for 60 hours, would have to hold three men for over 90 hours!

Once they were within an hour of the earth's atmosphere, they would crawl back to the command module, nicknamed Odyssey. Meanwhile, they continued to try and maintain themselves and their spaceship.

But the men on board Apollo 13 were worried. They weren't sure just how much damage had been done in the service module. Their supplies of oxygen and water, both vital for their continued survival, were kept in this section of the spacecraft. Although the plan chosen indicated that both water and oxygen would last long enough for the trip home, there was still the possibility of error. And if error occurred, the three men would be marooned forever in open space!

The plan engineered by Mission Control went into action on April 14, 1970, as the race to save the three astronauts before their supplies ran out, continued. The spaceship completed a circle around the moon. About 9,500 km (6,000 miles) from the right side of the moon, the crew began the crucial 4-minute, 24-second rocket firing that would send them on a course toward earth and an emergency splashdown in the Pacific Ocean.

Back in Texas, Mrs. Lovell and Mrs. Haise quietly awaited their husbands' return. Four-year-old Jeffrey Lovell continued to go to his school - wanting to be every bit as brave as his dad. All were confident that the people at Mission Control could successfully rescue their loved ones.

Then, the crucial time was upon them. The Apollo 13 was within an hour and a half of splashdown. Any mistakes now and the astronauts would be lost! The three of them crawled back to the command ship, saying farewell to their lifeboat - Aquarius. They prepared themselves to re-enter earth's atmosphere. This process had to be carried out with precision and control. They had to discard the service and lunar modules from the command module. If either one remained attached, the fuels in them would explode during re-entry, and the astronauts would be doomed!

At the critical moment, the world held its breath. The moment passed: the astronauts were safe! All over the world people forgot their differences as they joined together in happiness that these three great men had been saved.

G·WEIN

Rescue In Assisi

Written by Bob Goodwin
Illustrated by Eugene Pawczuk

It was midnight, September, 1943, in the small Italian town of Assisi. One of the most daring and heroic rescues of World War II was about to take place. It would start with only ten frightened people and eventually swell to over three hundred, with many more thousands helped to safety through the efforts of a small handful of men.

World War II was a horrible time; millions of men, women and children were killed. Adolf Hitler and his Nazi Party were the leaders of Germany. Hitler was especially hateful toward Jews. During World War II, he ordered his secret police, the Gestapo, to gather millions of Jews into huge death camps where they were killed. This is known as the Holocaust.

During World War II, Italy was occupied by Nazi troops. In 1943, the Allied armies of Great Britain, Canada and the United States invaded Italy, driving the Nazis back to Germany. The Gestapo began a savage round-up of Italian Jews in an effort to kill them all before the Allied armies arrived. Pope Pius XII, the leader of the Roman Catholic Church, secretly ordered all of his cardinals and bishops to rescue the Italian Jews from the Nazis. He gave orders to hide these hunted people in the churches, monasteries and convents of Italy, saving over thirty thousand people from the horrors of death camps.

The rescues began in Assisi. Two hooded figures crossed the square, their leather-soled sandals slapping the old, worn-out stones as they hurried off to their destination. They arrived in front of a large, beautifully decorated house. Next door was the Church of Santa Maria Maggiore, the former Cathedral of Assisi, Italy. The two men stepped up to the heavy oak door of the house and knocked. An old lady appeared, glancing nervously about at the darkness before letting the men inside. The lights in the house were out except for one room at the end of a long, thickly carpeted corridor. The lady motioned one of the men to wait by the doorway while she escorted the other down the darkened hall. The man followed her to the dimly lit room, knocked once, then waited.

Father Rufino Niccacci, priest of the Franciscan monastery of San Damiano, entered the room. Inside sat His Excellency, Giuseppe Nicolini, Bishop of Assisi, Italy. He told Father Niccacci that he was needed to undertake a very important job. Some people staying in the Bishop's house were in danger of losing their lives. The Bishop explained to Father Niccacci that these people were refugees, Jews who had just escaped from the Nazis in Rome. They needed help to escape before the Nazis found them.

Father Niccacci agreed that these people must be saved. The Bishop then told him that he must be the one to help them. Father Niccacci wondered how he would undertake this great challenge.

The rescue operation that helped save thousands of these people began here, in Assisi, with the Bishop and Father Niccacci. In response to his Bishop's plea, Father Niccacci organized a secret printing operation that produced false identification papers for the escaping Jews. These papers stated that the person carrying them was a Christian, thus avoiding arrest by the Gestapo. Thousands of these false identification papers were printed in Assisi and sent throughout Italy, saving countless numbers of people.

In Assisi itself, Father Niccacci personally saved the lives of over 300 Jews. He escorted them to the coastal city of Genoa in northern Italy, and helped them board ships for America. At times they were stopped by the Gestapo. Father Niccacci would have the people show their false papers, stating they were Christians returning from a religious visit to Assisi. They were never caught.

The Gestapo never knew that Father Niccacci was secretly rescuing Jews, even though the Germans occupied Assisi until 1944. If they had, Father Niccacci surely would have been killed.

Assisi is the birthplace of Francis, the great saint of the Roman Catholic Church. St. Francis of Assisi is beloved by millions of people around the world for his simplicity and love for all things. Father Rufino Niccacci, who died in 1977, was a modern-day Francis of Assisi, sheltering his suffering brothers and sisters from harm.

14

The Wrath of Hurricane Hazel

Written by Teri Kelly
Illustrated by Vickie Rowden

On October 15, 1954, Joe Ward walked home from work as he always did, crossing the wooden bridge over the Humber River in Toronto, Canada. Joe hadn't bothered with the weather warnings of Hurricane Hazel due to hit Toronto that afternoon; after all, how often did hurricanes hit Canada? But the rains continued, much more than 63-year-old Joe and his wife, Annie, could ever remember. Joe had never seen the peaceful Humber River swell and rage with such fury. The storm started in the Caribbean on October 6, 1954, and ripped through the eastern coast of the United States before hitting Toronto nine days later. Tons of water flooded Toronto and $25 million worth of property was demolished.

On Raymore Drive in Toronto, on the night of the hurricane, Annie went to bed at 9 p.m., but Joe stayed up and finally fell asleep on the couch. When he awoke around midnight, Joe moved slowly from the couch, placing his feet on the floor. He was startled to find he was knee-deep in water. He splashed to the front door to find chaos and destruction everywhere. Willow trees were uprooted, his beloved rose gardens had vanished, and water from the raging Humber was gushing through the streets at a tremendous speed. Joe slammed his front door shut and ran to open his basement door, to find his beloved English terrier, Lassie, swimming toward him. He gathered Lassie into his arms and waded through the water to wake his sleeping wife.

Joe made a hole in the ceiling and the three climbed to the shingled roof. The roof broke free of the house and the Wards drifted, as though on a raft, down their street. Their roof smashed into their neighbor, Jack Anderson's roof, which thankfully was still attached to the house. The Wards climbed onto the Anderson roof, and for seven hours clung to the TV aerial with all their strength. The dirty brown water rose higher as it crashed forward, destroying everything in its path. Joe placed his own cold body over his wife's in a vain attempt to keep her warm.

Dawn was breaking and the Wards could see in the violet sky, a red hydro helicopter. It hovered over them. Finally, the crew were able to transport them safely off the roof. They were saved!

The Andrea Doria

Written by Peter Robertson
Illustrated by Tim Zeltner

Linda Morgan, a slender, brown-haired fourteen-year-old, was one of the 1,706 passengers aboard the magnificent *Andrea Doria*. She shared the enthusiasm of everyone else traveling on the cruise ship. Ten large decks, stretching 200 meters from bow (front) to stern (rear), contained four dining rooms, two theaters, two lounges, three swimming pools, two ballrooms, two stores and a chapel. With all of this, passengers taking the trans-Atlantic voyage from Europe to North America had always enjoyed themselves. Now on the 101st journey of the *Andrea Doria*, Captain Piero Calamai was sure this trip would also be an exciting one. However, he couldn't have known that in only a short time this excitement would change to terror.

17

Linda was particularly excited a few days into the journey. That evening, the Captain was expected to join her family's table in the dining room. She looked forward to adding his signature to her autograph book that already contained the names of Jimmy Stewart, Gregory Peck and Cary Grant. Unfortunately for Linda, this encounter would never take place.

The Captain was forced to remain in command on the bridge, as huge fog drifts were beginning to cover everything and made traveling difficult. Considering the thickness of the fog, the *Andrea Doria* was traveling too quickly.

Fog was known to sailors as the "quiet killer of the sea." It could make a ship seem invisible, as though a dark blanket had been lowered over it. Even with the aid of highly sophisticated radar systems, fog remains a deadly villain to any ship. More ocean vessels have fallen prey to fog than to storms, coral reefs or icebergs.

Captain Calamai sounded the whistle. The ship's foghorn immediately began to bellow its signal. The fog signal was a blast that pierced the air for six seconds and was repeated every minute and forty seconds thereafter.

It was 10:45 p.m. Eastern daylight time, July 25, 1956, when Senior Second Officer Curzio Franchini first sighted a vessel advancing toward them on his radar. The approaching ship was the *Stockholm* , a powerful vessel designed to break through ice. Franchini watched intently as the bright green bar of the radar moved through its normal circular pattern. Each time it revolved, it showed a small bean-shaped object, referred to as a pip.

The approaching vessel was about 28 kilometers (17 miles) away; almost directly in line with the *Andrea Doria*. Franchini continued to monitor the radar, deciding that, if both ships maintained their present course, they would safely pass on the starboard side (right). When two ships are approaching each other from opposite directions, they are supposed to pass port-to-port (left), unless this would force them into a crossing course.

By this time, the fog had grown so thick that the bow of the ship was barely visible from the bridge. Captain Calamai had to strain to see through his binoculars in search of the *Stockholm* masthead lights. The lights appeared blurred at first, but became brighter as the seconds passed.

Captain Calamai felt his body go cold with terror. He realized the *Stockholm* was on a direct collision course with his beautiful ship. The *Stockholm* was trying to pass on the port side, while the *Andrea Doria* was trying to pass on the starboard side. A collision couldn't be avoided!

Seconds later, at 11:10 p.m., it happened! The bow of the *Stockholm* cut into the exposed starboard side of the *Andrea Doria*. The shriek of metal scraping against metal echoed into the night. Sparks of fire showered the surface of the water below. The *Stockholm* pushed its way ten meters (30 feet) into the belly of the *Andrea Doria*. Finally, the *Stockholm* came to a halt.

The assault on the *Andrea* was more crippling than it would have been because the bow of the *Stockholm* was reinforced with heavy thick steel plating. This had enabled the Swedish ship to follow icebreakers through the frozen waters of Scandinavia. Now it had destroyed the *Andrea Doria*.

As the *Stockholm* reversed and pulled away from the *Andrea,* thousands of tons of ocean water rushed in, invading the vacant holes. The crews on both vessels responded to orders, reacting instantly in an attempt to keep their ships afloat. SOS signals were transmitted immediately.

The *Ile de France*, a gigantic French cruiseship, received the SOS. However, the ship was far from the accident site. Would the *Ile de France* be able to reach the sinking *Andrea Doria* in time?

Meanwhile, the U.S. coast guard began its own rescue procedure, sending out cutters from various ports along the eastern seaboard. Unfortunately, they couldn't send out planes or helicopters right away because the fog made it difficult to find the *Andrea*.

The passengers on the *Andrea* were becoming very frightened. By now, most of them were making their way to the upper decks. Some of the men were linking hands, forming a human chain, pulling older passengers up from the lower decks.

Linda Morgan's sleeping quarters were directly above the point where the *Stockholm* hit. As the bow of the *Stockholm* pulled away from the *Andrea*, it carried Linda (still lying in her bed) with it and left her lying on the open deck of the *Stockholm*, just above its crushed bow. Unconscious, Linda didn't know what had happened. Shortly afterward, she woke and, in a stunned voice, called out for her mother and father. Becoming very confused and frightened, Linda realized something awful had happened. Finally, a member of the crew on the *Stockholm* heard Linda calling. He rushed to her and covered her cold body with warm blankets. She had survived the nightmare!

Back on the *Andrea Doria*, most of the passengers had gone to the upper decks. Panic and terror were felt by all as they waited for the lifeboats to be lowered. However, the lifeboats on both sides of the *Andrea* couldn't be lowered because the hull was tilted at a severe angle, and the launching apparatus was useless. All that could be done now was to wait for help!

The *Stockholm*, after dealing with its own damage, was now confident it would remain afloat. It sent out lifeboats to aid in the rescue. By this time, the coast guard, along with several smaller cruiseships, had reached the battered *Andrea Doria*. They removed the passengers as fast as they could. It was a slow and awkward process, with the threat of the *Andrea* capsizing any moment growing greater as the minutes passed.

Finally, the *Ile de France* arrived. In heroic fashion, the crew rescued 753 passengers. It wasn't until early the following morning, eleven hours after the collision, that the *Andrea Doria* finally gave in to the ocean it once ruled. Twenty-nine thousand tons of steel and nine million man-hours of labor went down in a whisper.

Miraculously, 1,655 passengers survived, thanks to the captains and crews of ships such as the *Ile de France*, *W.H. Thomas*, and *Cape Ann*. Most of the 51 fatalities happened at the moment of impact. The collision between the *Andrea Doria* and the *Stockholm* is one of the most tragic sea disasters recorded. It is, however, thanks to the courageous men and women involved, one of the greatest sea rescues ever.

SECONDS TO GO

Written by Monique Hammel
Illustrated by Greg Joy

Michelle Dejesus looked with wide eyes at the crowds of people swarming around her. Holding her hand firmly, her mother led her through the turnstile. The subway station was filled with travelers on their way to take the evening train home from another busy day. Cute four-year-old Michelle was pushed up the stairs and onto the platform with her mother Joanne and her Aunt Margarita, as the surging crowd carried them along.

The three stopped a few feet from the platform's edge and waited for the next local train, which would arrive in a couple of minutes. But Michelle could not stand still. Pulling her hand from her mother's grip, she skipped to the edge of the platform and looked down the tracks, hoping to catch a glimpse of the coming train. As she peered into the darkened tunnel, she leaned forward. Suddenly, she felt her foot slip. She lost her balance and fell, landing hard on the tracks below! She lay still, stunned by the fall - directly in the path of the train!

On the platform above her someone screamed. Confused exclamations of horror and shouts for help rang out in the tunnel as the onlookers realized what had happened. A hundred people stood paralyzed, staring down at the tiny figure. Among them was 34-year-old Everett Sanderson, standing close to where Michelle lay, and Miguel Maisonette, a short distance from her, at the other end of the platform.

It was as if time stood still on that platform in the 86th Street subway station in New York. Precious seconds were ticking away as everyone waited for someone else to do something.

Then, two things happened to break the spell. A low grumble rose in the tunnel and a sudden breeze swept across the platform. The train was coming! At the same time, a small voice cried from the tracks, calling for her mother. Michelle was waking up!

Suddenly, two men jumped onto the tracks and began running toward her. Miguel Maisonette ran smoothly, jumping between the railway ties and over the rails with an ease that came from years of playing dangerous games of dare as a boy on these same tracks. Everett Sanderson moved more awkwardly, sweating in his coat. But desperation gave him speed - he knew he had to try to rescue the little girl.

As the two men raced toward her, the rumble of the train grew louder. It would be at the station any second! Just then, Miguel saw that there was someone else on the tracks - Everett - trying to get to Michelle, too. In a flash he realized that the other man would reach the girl first, so without breaking his stride or slackening speed, he turned off to the side, grabbed the platform with his hands and threw himself up over the edge. Once safe, he moved quickly up the platform until he was across from Michelle. There he knelt, muscles tense, held out his arms - and waited.

Everett had not seen Miguel. All he could see was Michelle. As he raced toward her, what everyone had been dreading, happened! The ground began to shake, the rumble rose to a deafening roar and the train appeared!

Everett didn't stop. He was almost at Michelle. Suddenly, there was a screech of metal and a shower of sparks as the driver of the train slammed on the emergency brakes. The train slowed, but it was too late! It could never stop in time! It looked like Everett was Michelle's only hope.

With the wheels screaming and the huge train skidding ever closer to him, Everett lunged desperately for Michelle, grabbing her with one hand. Then, in a burst of strength, he lifted her and threw her onto the platform where Miguel caught her, tumbling over backward. Michelle was saved!

But Everett was in trouble. The train loomed right in front of him. At this speed, it would be upon him in just seconds. Hurling himself to the side of the tracks, Everett grabbed the edge of the platform and tried to jump up. His chest hit the wall and he was knocked back. The train was screaming toward him! Everett had one more chance to save his life. He didn't think he was going to make it.

Rex Johnson, a patrol officer on his beat in the station, Michelle's aunt and Miguel crouched on the platform near him. As Everett reached up to try one last jump, they grabbed him by the coat and arms and pulled, snatching him out of the way just as the train thundered past!

Everett Sanderson was a hero. And today, a small mark on the edge of his shoe made by the train reminds him of January 16, 1975, when he saved Michelle Dejesus' life, and came so close to losing his own.

KANGO AND THE FLYING DOCTOR

Written by Janet Stewart
Illustrated by Rick Rowden

Six-year-old Kango lay almost unconscious in an outback station in Western Australia. His tummy was swollen more than twice its normal size, and he looked more dead than alive. His mother, Josie, was standing anxiously nearby, wondering what had happened to her little Kango. Only days ago, he had been hopping and running about like the kangaroos for which he was named. Now he lay so very still!

The nurse at the outback station knew there wasn't much hope for Kango. His appendix had burst, and the poison was moving quickly through his small body. Here in the wilderness of the outback, there was only one person who could save Kango: The Flying Doctor!

The emergency service of the Royal Flying Doctor began in 1912 with Reverend John Flynn. With a landmass of over 8,000,000 square kilometers, the continent of Australia had many isolated areas. Flynn knew that the natives of this vast country needed help. Frequently, the nearest doctor would be over 800 kilometers away, and messengers on horseback had to cross treacherous sand-bogs and water barriers. Flynn thought that many tragedies could be avoided if planes could be used to cross the great expanses of land and bring medical assistance to the people of the outback. He was right! The first year the Flying Doctor was in service, in 1928, over 32,000 kilometers were traveled, and 225 people were rescued from the claws of death.

In 1957, the Flying Doctor had been operating for 29 years. And on the day that Kango desperately needed him, one of the Flying Doctors was in Darwin taking calls from the outback.

When the call came through, Dr. George Sava, a visiting surgeon from England, was ready. Knowing from the nurse's description that Kango was seriously ill, he quickly gathered his equipment and boarded the waiting plane. With the Flying Doctor Service, no one in Australia was more than two hours away from help in an emergency.

When George reached the station, he saw that the boy was close to death. In his mind, he thought that this was surely a hopeless case. But he was a doctor, and he would do his best! He gave Kango an injection of medicine to numb the pain. Then, as quickly as possible, they readied Kango for his trip to hospital for the operation that might save his life.

But Kango's mother, Josie, was an aborigine of Australia and having lived her whole life in the barren outback, she was unfamiliar with modern medicine. She was afraid to let Kango go with these strangers to a 'hospital.' Crucial time was being lost! Finally, George convinced Josie that they were her son's only chance for survival.

With Josie in tow, they boarded the plane and flew to the hospital in Darwin. George had already made the necessary arrangements they would need at the hospital from the radio in the plane. When they arrived everything was ready.

As Dr. Sava scrubbed in preparation for the operation, he felt sick! How could he save this little boy who was already so close to death? Knowing that Kango was named after the energetic kangaroos made Dr. Sava sad to think that Kango would never again be like his namesake.

He began the operation. Cutting Kango's stomach, he drained the poison from inside him. When he had done all he could, Dr. Sava wheeled Kango out. He was alive and now all they could do was wait.

Days passed. Then about a week later, Dr. Sava went to check on Kango. He was awake and out of danger. The heroic Flying Doctor Service had saved another life!

25

Control Tower Fire

Written by Teri Kelly
Illustrated by Gary Wein

It was 9:45 p.m. on November 4th, 1958. Marcel Courtoy and Guillaume Michaux were at their usual stations in Brussel's airport control tower. It was an average evening for the two controllers. Nothing out of the ordinary had occurred - until they both smelled smoke!

A kerosene lamp had exploded, sparking an uncontrolled fire in the control tower. Stationed almost 50 meters (155 feet) above ground level, the two men immediately thought of how they could escape to safety. But to do that would mean instant danger for the incoming aircraft. Their responsibility was to the innocent passengers aboard the incoming planes. The controlmen were trapped!

The fire alarm was blaring throughout the building. Eleven minutes had passed since they first smelled smoke, and already it was too late to reach safety. The tower was ablaze! No longer could they even escape the smoke in their glassed-in tower.

To avoid instant death, the two men jumped to the roof below. Smoke was belching from all the windows, and flames seared up the elevator shafts. The two men thought they had met their end! Below them, a mob of hysterical onlookers gathered, while firefighters frantically tried to raise a ladder to save the trapped men, only to find it wasn't long enough to reach them.

Fortunately, the control tower also had a helicopter hangar. Marcel Courtoy shouted to the firemen below to send for a helicopter. Armand Adam, a helicopter maintenance manager, was summoned at once. Hearing of the two men's plight, Adam gathered a heavy rope and shoulder harness, and attached the rope to the cabin seats of the helicopter. His idea was to hover over the tower while suspending the rope and attached harness to the trapped men on the tower. They would place the harness around their bodies, and the helicopter would carry them to safety.

Pilot Gerard Tremerie, with the aid of assistant Charles Gillet, and Adam, immediately boarded the helicopter for the rescue mission. Moments later, the three rescuers were directly over the fire and could see that heat and wind were so great that the rope-and-harness technique would have to be abandoned.

The two trapped men were barely conscious. Tremerie had difficulty landing the helicopter as the tower roof was badly weakened by the fire. The helicopter blades continued to turn to keep the craft's weight off the damaged roof. The tower men were confused and disoriented. Adam and Gillet climbed from the helicopter to aid the two victims through the doors of the helicopter.

Only 45 minutes had passed since Courtoy and Michaux first smelled smoke. The rescue mission was a success!

TRAPPED BY ICE

Written by Janet Stewart
Illustrated by Rick Rowden

William McKinlay huddled in his ice house trying to keep warm. He found it difficult to believe that at 25 years old he was stranded in the Arctic. Not very long ago, he had been teaching mathematics and science at a school in Glasgow, Scotland. Now he was on Wrangle Island, north of Siberia, marooned with 22 other men, one woman, two children, sixteen dogs, and a little black cat named Nigeraurak. Of these people, thirteen were scientists from Canada, Scotland, the United States, Australia, New Zealand, Denmark, Norway, and France. They were all part of Vilhjalmur Stefansson's expedition to explore the Arctic. And here they sat, waiting for someone to save them.

The group had left Vancouver, Canada, on June 17, 1913, on board the *Karluk*, a twenty-year-old, 250-ton whaling ship. The skipper of the *Karluk*, Captain Robert Bartlett, had warned everyone before setting out that the *Karluk* wasn't strong enough to take the pressure of the Arctic ice. There were too many crates below the deck of the ship, and 150 crates on deck made the *Karluk* sit so deep in the water its deck was almost level with the sea. The Captain's warnings went unheeded, and the ship set off.

As the *Karluk* went through the Bering Strait into the open Arctic, William and the others could feel the force and power of the screeching wind. They anchored near Point Hope, Alaska, and visited the Eskimo village of Tigerak where they bought skins and boots and hired two Eskimos as hunters and dog drivers.

They set off from Point Hope on August 1, 1913. It was snowing and temperatures were well below freezing. The next day, William saw his first ice pack: A large area of water covered over with ice. The ship's captain couldn't find an opening or break through the ice, so they had to head south, away from their destination.

Then, on August 3, they tried again to find an opening, but failed. Finally, the wind changed and moved the ice; the *Karluk* pushed through. As evening approached, the ice pack closed around the ship again. The ice was so heavily packed that the ship came to a dead stop! As William looked around at the broken, rough ice surrounding them, he thought it looked like huge, glistening marble blocks. Along with some of the other scientists, he left the *Karluk* and played on the ice until 4 a.m., forgetting the time, since August in the Arctic has almost 24 hours of light.

On August 6, the *Karluk* broke through the ice, but shortly after, the ship's steering broke down. To be without steering in an ice pack meant serious trouble! After two hours of work, the steering was fixed, but by this time the ice had closed in around the ship again.

Through the month of August and into September, the *Karluk* drifted with the ice pack to the northwest. Everyone on board was getting restless and bored. The scientists wanted to start their work exploring the Arctic, but as long as they were stuck in ice, they couldn't do anything. The crew were tired of the scientists on board; they thought scientists were useless when it came to running the ship.

The drifting finally stopped, and the ship, still surrounded by ice, was close to land. Stefansson decided to go over the ice for a few days, with a sledge, some of the dogs and a couple of Eskimos to do a little hunting.

After he left, a gale came up, and the ice between shore and the ship split. The *Karluk* was carried away by the wind. Drifting snow made it impossible to see anything, and all they could do was wait for the storm to stop. Meanwhile, after returning to find the *Karluk* gone, Stefansson traveled to a nearby Eskimo village where he rested until another ship arrived.

The storm ended in early October, but the ship remained locked in the ice pack. One day, William saw open water to the south of the ship, but there was no way they could reach it. Then one night William and the others heard a strange noise. It was a noise like thunder, made from the pressure of ice pushing on ice. The Captain had everyone move supplies onto the ice around the ship. He knew the *Karluk* would soon be crushed. To survive they would have to abandon ship!

They made shelters on the ice with the crates from the ship and put snow around the crates to keep out the cold wind. They stayed aboard the *Karluk*, waiting for the time when the ice would crush and sink it, while the dogs stayed in the shelters.

On December 26, the ice began to crack under the pressure. The crew and scientists began to abandon their ship. By this time, they had drifted close to Wrangle Island, north of Siberia. Once they left their ship, they would have to try and reach Wrangle Island and then Siberia.

A few days later, on January 2, 1914, in the middle of a terrible storm, they waited on the ice pack, in their shelters, while the ice crushed the *Karluk*. Water rushed into the hull and the ship tilted over on its side. When the storm ended on January 21, the Captain sent two groups of men to find Wrangle Island. They weren't sure which way to go, but hoped they would make it.

Two more parties left the ice pack on February 19. One of the men had Nigeraurak, the cat, in a bag on his back. They were over 100 kilometers from Wrangle Island and had to struggle through freezing-cold temperatures and huge blocks of ice (sometimes as high as 30 meters) to reach the island. When they stopped to rest, they built an igloo (a house made from snow) to shelter them from the fierce wind.

Not all of them made it! Those who did made shelters, hunted, and built fires to keep warm. They were all exhausted and couldn't even think of trying to reach Siberia. It was March 12, 1914 - eight months since they had begun their voyage. Finally, the Captain decided he would take seven of the dogs, a sledge, and an Eskimo and go to Siberia for help. If he didn't leave soon, he wouldn't have the strength to go and they wouldn't survive. His success was their only hope!

After the Captain left, the rest of the men did what they could, hunting for food and keeping warm. Their diet was poor and many of them got frostbite from the freezing temperatures. Months went by and they were almost out of ammunition. William McKinlay was worried: How could they survive when their guns no longer worked and their food was gone? Several of the scientists had already died, and the rest of them were close to starvation. They wondered if they would last another winter in the Arctic.

August ended, and with September came heavy snow and cold winds. They had given up hope of ever being rescued. Then, on September 7, 1914, they spotted a ship steaming toward them. They shouted and screamed and someone shot off a gun. The ship really was coming closer! On deck was their captain; he had made it to Siberia after all!

SPRINGHILL COAL MINE DISASTER

Written by Teri Kelly
Illustrated by Vickie Rowden

A disastrous explosion ripped through the coal mine in Springhill, Nova Scotia, Canada, in 1956. Twenty-six men were buried alive below the surface. In the wake of the tragedy, the Cumberlain Railway and Coal Company sealed the shaft.

But the miners of Springhill were desperate men who would find themselves unemployed and their families poor if the mines were closed. They petitioned to have the mines reopened. The town council also requested to have the mines operating to avoid Springhill becoming a ghost town.

Reluctantly, the Cumberlain Railway and Coal Company opened its deepest mine - shaft Number 2. All Springhill miners once again boarded the "rake cars" at a 45-degree slope into the bowels of the earth. Down they rode, deep below the earth's surface to mine coal in the gassy tunnels.

The afternoon of Thursday, October 23, 1958, didn't seem any different to the miners ready to start their 3 p.m. to 11 p.m. shift. It was a bright, warm, cloudless afternoon, and the miners complained of having to descend the pit on such a lovely day. Reluctantly, they put on their mining shirts, overalls, plastic helmets and steel-toed safety boots. Each miner was given a safety lamp containing a freshly charged battery that would supply light for ten hours. They filled their water cans and rode the rake cars to the tunnels far below the ground.

At 8 p.m., the most devastating earthquake hit the Number 2 mining shaft. A surge of hot air pushed against the tunnels of the mines below. With a crashing, thunderous roar, the blast heaved upward, caving in the roofs of the mine's tunnels. The shock of the earth's inner tremor was felt in neighboring towns.

The local townspeople knew from previous experience what this sudden jolt meant. Frantically, they ran to the mines, hopes high. Rescue workers, with heavy oxygen equipment fixed to their backs, descended the devastated mine. The tunnels were packed with debris, and the rescue workers had to crawl on their bellies, slowly digging along the way. The rescue workers themselves were in great danger as they could choke to death from poisonous methane gas in the mines.

Two of the first survivors, Henry Dykens and Tommy McManaman, heard an enormous roar, like a canon shot. The next thing they knew, they were both buried in coal up to their noses. Tommy wiggled and clawed himself free, then went to help Henry. They scratched along through the tunnel where they spotted another miner, Keith Cummings, buried to his waist in coal. There was no time to lose! They yanked Keith from the debris, broken leg and all, and carried him along the tunnel before the gases poisoned them.

One by one, the survivors surfaced to the top of the pit where makeshift hospitals were set up to tend the injured. A "tag-board" with numbered brass tags representing each miner was posted, and as they surfaced, the tag was removed from the board, showing the miner was alive.

By noon on Friday, October 24, eighty-one "live" nametags were removed from the board. As night fell, the rescue workers were not having much success finding more survivors. But the families of the miners still trapped in the mines refused to give up hope. Friday slipped into Saturday, then Sunday, Monday, and Tuesday. The miners' families stayed close by in tents, praying for the safety of their husbands and fathers. On Wednesday, the sixth day after the explosion, 69 men were still trapped in the mine. Television and newspaper reporters had given up hope and left. But the rescue workers refused to do the same! They worked around the clock in crews of 70 men, digging and clawing through the rubble, hour after hour.

At 2 p.m. on Wednesday, Blair Phillips, the mine's supervisor, who was testing for methane gas, heard a faint, muffled sound coming from a pipe sticking out of the rubble. Phillips shouted back and heard a faint cry for water. There were twelve men still trapped behind a block of solid rock. They had spent six days trapped in a very small space. The rescue workers dug for twelve hours to blast out a tunnel for the men to pass through.

Outside the mine, an excited shout was heard after learning there were still survivors in the mine. The rescue team shoved a copper tube through the ventilator pipe and poured down water, hot coffee and soup.

By 4:30 Thursday morning, after six days and eight hours of entombment, the twelve survivors made their way to the surface. The crowds broke into thunderous cheers as each man was removed by stretcher.

Seven miners were still not accounted for. Finally, after nine days of being trapped, the next survivors made their way to freedom early Saturday morning. Of the 174 miners trapped beneath the earth, 99 men were miraculously saved. The Springhill coal mine never reopened.

THE HUMAN BRIDGE

Written by Janet Stewart   *Illustrated by Greg Joy*

Andrew Parker, his wife Eleanor, and their twelve-year-old daughter, Janice, decided to take a day trip March 6, 1987, from Dover, England, to Zeebrugge, Belgium, aboard the 8,000-ton *Herald of Free Enterprise* car ferry.

But the day ended tragically when the ferry capsized just off the Belgian port of Zeebrugge. Panic set in as hundreds of people tried to escape. Andrew, his family, and about sixteen others were trapped on one side of what used to be a corridor when the ferry was upright. Now, with the ferry on its side, the corridor had become a chasm that had to be crossed if they were to survive.

While everyone around him was losing control, Andrew calmly thought about what he could do to help. A rope had been lowered through a porthole for them to climb up, but first they had to cross the chasm. Time was precious as the ferry continued to fill up with water. Then Andrew had an idea. He lowered his 6-foot, 3-inch frame across the opening, and his wife and daughter slowly crawled over him. Continuing to lay there, the rest of the survivors crossed over, using Andrew's body as a bridge.

Once on the other side, they looked up at the dangling rope. It seemed an impossible task for them to climb it. Rather than give up hope, Andrew thought of a solution. Realizing from his school days how difficult it was to shinny up a rope, Andrew helped refashion the rope into a pully. Starting with the lightest people, the rescuers pulled them up, one by one.

Finally, it was Andrew's turn, but he was too heavy to haul up. After helping all the others, Andrew was left alone. Then someone found a ladder and passed it down to Andrew. With great relief he slowly climbed to the top -- and safety! Once at the top, Andrew looked down at his arms in amazement! There, clutched to his chest, was a tiny baby! Andrew had no idea how it had gotten there or whose it was. The baby was another of the lucky people Andrew had saved.

The Raging Volturno

Written by Bob Goodwin
Illustrated by Tim Zeltner

Imagine saving people from a raging fire with tons of inflammable oil. It actually happened, years ago, in the middle of the Atlantic Ocean. It was October 10, 1913, and a large ocean liner, the *Volturno*, was on fire.

Making a sea journey from Rotterdam, Holland, to Halifax, Canada, the *Volturno* had over 600 passengers and crew. Many of those on board were eastern European farmers leaving their old homeland in Russia to settle in western Canada. Most of the men, women and children were poor, anxious to begin their lives as Canadian farmers. In the middle of the cold, dark Atlantic Ocean, their dream would turn into a nightmare.

The journey started on October 2, a day of calm seas and bright, blue skies. Six days later, the weather turned bad! Gale-force winds and freezing rain assaulted the liner as she made her crossing. Mountainous seas slammed furiously into the side of the ship, rolling her about like a cork in a duck pond.

Inside the ship, deep in the holds, were steel barrels of a chemical called barium oxide. A huge wave slammed the side of the *Volturno*, causing her to twist dangerously to one side. The barrels of barium oxide broke loose from their metal strappings and bounced about in the ship's hold. Several containers opened up, spilling the dangerous, highly flammable chemical.

Flames started in the bowels of the ship, spreading furiously as more barrels broke open with the tremendous heat. The alarm was raised and passengers scrambled to the deck. What they saw was not a welcome sight! Huge waves towered above the ship; stinging pellets of ice and rain hit people huddled on the deck. Death stalked the poor, trapped passengers of the *Volturno*. There was no escape! Children clung tightly to their parents as they watched in hopeless fear.

In desperation, the captain of the *Volturno*, Francis Inch, decided to try and save the people by putting them into lifeboats and lowering them into the sea. The *Volturno* was well-equipped with lifeboats. It was only eighteen months since the huge ocean liner, the *Titanic*, struck an iceberg in the North Atlantic and went down, carrying over 1,500 people to an icy grave. The *Titanic* had only enough lifeboats for one-third of her passengers. The owners of the *Volturno* didn't want the same thing to happen to their ship. They made sure that every passenger on board could be saved by stocking the ship with many lifeboats. What they didn't count on was the weather!

Captain Inch ordered the boats to be stocked with food and blankets. Number two lifeboat was the first to be lowered into the rough sea. It touched the water and immediately capsized!

Everyone was swept away. Number three and fifteen were sent next. A huge wave struck the two lifeboats half-way down the side of the ship, smashing them against the steel hull. Men, women and children disappeared. Number six was lowered. Captain Inch thought that he had finally managed it. The next instant, he watched in horror as a wave carried off the tiny boat. All seemed lost! The Captain ordered his radio operator, Mr. Seddon, to send a continuous SOS message. During the night, a number of ships pulled within sight of the *Volturno*.

Nine rescue ships, carrying over 5,000 people, anchored close by, anxiously watching the drama. As night closed in, the big liners turned their huge floodlights on the *Volturno*, picking out the survivors huddled together. Smoke and fire belched continuously from inside the ship. Captain Inch radioed the rescue ships for help, but nothing could be done until daybreak. The passengers on board the *Volturno* sang hymns and prayed for a miracle.

Dawn broke, October 11 - a bleak, raw, stormy day with strong winds and high seas. Several attempts were made by the rescue ships to get lifeboats and cables across to the *Volturno*, but all failed. The seas were simply too rough. The fire inside the *Volturno* was now spreading up to the deck. The steel plating under their feet grew hot, causing the passengers to jump from one foot to the other. Several people looked over the side of the ship, but pulled back in fear of the monstrous waves. It seemed like the end! Then a miracle happened!

The Anglo-American Oil Company tanker *Narragansett,* loaded with 3,000 metric tons of lubricating oil, pulled alongside the burning ship. Orders were given and the crew of the tanker opened her holds, spilling the oil into the sea. Oil will float on the surface of the water, weighing it down and causing a temporary calm. The oil slick spread in a wide arc, smoothing out the seas and giving the rescue ships a chance to lower their lifeboats. It was a risky maneuver, but it worked! The rescue ships saved 521 lives, thanks to the calming action of the heavy lubricating oil from the *Narragansett.*

The Bogie Drop

Illustrated by Denis Gagne

Inglis and Doole were experienced mountain climbers. November 15, 1982, after climbing to a ridge as part of their training with Mt. Cook's Search and Rescue Team, they ended up in an ice cave. They had enough food for one night, so they decided to spend it in the cave. When they started to leave the next morning, the pair faced howling winds, rain, cloud and snow. They were stuck in a white-out which was to last for most of the next two weeks. Winds were as high as 80 knots and it was snowing heavily. The conditions that kept Inglis and Doole trapped also prevented their close friends at the Mt. Cook Rescue Team from finding them.

After eight days, hope of finding the men alive started to fade. Then, unexpectedly, Doole and Inglis were spotted standing near the entrance to their ice cave. A helicopter crew had seen them but the machine couldn't land safely on the 3,764-meter-high mountain. The next morning, a helicopter crew prepared to take off. They stopped at the Empress Shelf, where climbers were waiting to attach a rope and harness to the bottom of the helicopter. Don Bogie, senior rescue mountaineer, got into the harness and hung below the helicopter. In the next moments Pilot Small demonstrated all his flying skills. He hovered above the ice cave and placed Bogie in exactly the right position to plunge down through the ice hole and rescue the two men. Suddenly, ice was all around Bogie as he swayed on the end of the rope. Then, he was gone!

The drop had worked, and he found himself down a hole in the ice, inside a long ice cave. More importantly, he found the two men who had been at the center of New Zealand's attention for a fortnight. Phil Doole and Mark Inglis were freezing cold, hungry and suffering from frostbitten feet: there was no time to waste. Bogie quickly put Mark Inglis into a stretcher attached to the helicopter rope, and the two men disappeared up the hole, through the icy air, into the waiting helicopter. Using the 'Bogie Drop' again, Don entered the cave and moved Doole onto the stretcher and up to the waiting helicopter to successfully rescue both men from the cave that had been their prison.

133 DAYS ADRIFT

Written by Diane Campbell
Illustrated by Denis Gagne

It was 1942 and the world was at war. In the fall of that year, the British Merchant ship *Ben Lomond* set sail from Cape Town, South Africa, with a crew of 55, including 25-year-old Second Steward Poon Lim, a native of Hainan Island, south of China. November 23, 1942, west of St. Paul Rocks in the South Atlantic, the *Ben Lomond* was torpedoed by a Nazi U-boat. Severely damaged by the attack, the freighter began to sink rapidly.

Reacting quickly to the situation, Poon Lim secured a life jacket around himself, jumped into the rolling sea, and swam away from the crippled vessel. Suddenly, the boilers of the *Ben Lomond* exploded and she disappeared into the depths of the Atlantic Ocean, silencing the cries for help from the other crew

Determined to stay alive, Poon Lim strained to keep his head above the waves as his eyes searched the water for a life raft. His two-hour battle to stay afloat ended when he spotted a life raft a few hundred meters away. Summoning all his remaining strength, he swam toward the small craft and clambered aboard, exhausted.

Sometime later, Poon Lim surveyed his small square wooden life raft and found it stocked with tins of British biscuits, a large jug of water, some flares, and a flashlight. He decided that if he limited his food intake to four biscuits a day, and his water intake to a few small swallows a day, his rations would last at least thirty days.

Each day he scanned the horizon for a ship that might rescue him. Twice his spirits soared when rescue seemed close. But, his frantic shouts and wild arm-waving were ignored, first by a freighter that passed not far from his raft, and then by a U.S. Navy patrol plane that flew over his tiny vessel. Another time, a German U-boat spotted him but continued on its way, choosing not to kill him. In deep despair, Poon Lim found these to be his loneliest times.

No longer anticipating assistance from others and with supplies running low, Poon Lim formulated a survival plan. To maintain his strength, he exercised twice a day by swimming around the raft, always keeping his eyes alert for sharks.

To catch rainwater, he made a container from the canvas covering of his life jacket. He fashioned a fish hook from a flashlight wire, using the water jug to shape the metal. The sturdy hemp rope in his raft became a fishing line, and a piece of biscuit served as bait. He finally caught a fish, ate it raw, and used the remains as bait to catch another meal. As the days passed, he caught a few more fish and found that if he laid them out in the sun to bake, their taste improved.

Toward the end of his second month adrift, he sighted some seagulls. Seizing the opportunity to vary his diet, he set about building a nest of matted seaweed. In it he placed some rotten fish, certain the smell would entice the birds closer to him. He lay still until a gull landed and attacked the fish. At once, the seaman jumped up and grasped the bird by its neck. The seagull viciously attacked Poon Lim with its strong beak and claws, causing him deep cuts and scratches. The battle won, Poon Lim put his mind to work again.

With great effort, he removed a nail from one of the raft's timbers, used this to tear a strip of metal from an empty biscuit tin, and then shaped the metal by beating it with his shoe. Then he sectioned the bird with the crude knife and, after taking his fill of fresh meat, cut the rest of the flesh into strips to serve as his food supply until he caught another seagull or fish.

Next, Poon Lim set out to catch one of the sharks he had spotted in the water around his raft. To prepare for the struggle he knew was coming, he braided the hemp rope to strengthen his fishing line and wrapped both of his hands in canvas from his life jacket. He used the remains of a bird as bait and tossed the line into the ocean. A relatively small shark, swallowed the bait. Once aboard the tiny craft, the shark attacked Poon Lim who finally subdued the vicious fish by striking it repeatedly with a seawater-filled jug.

On the side of his life raft, Poon Lim had carved out the number of days he had been adrift - notches marked the days and Xs the nights. On the 131st day alone at sea, he noticed some changes in his surroundings. The color of the ocean had changed from black to light green. Clumps of seaweed could be seen floating on top of the water, and a greater number of birds appeared in the sky. He was greatly encouraged by these signs which indicated he could be nearing land.

On April 5, 1943, four and a half months after climbing into the wooden raft, he spotted a small sailing vessel on the horizon. In an effort to gain the attention of the crew, he waved his arms wildly, jumped about and shouted for them to come to his aid. He became really excited when the fishing boat changed course and headed toward his tiny vessel. They picked Poon Lim up, and headed west toward Belem, a Brazilian port at the mouth of the Amazon River.

Poon Lim had drifted across the Atlantic Ocean in 133 days. Remarkably, he lost only twenty pounds. He was presented with the British Empire Medal, Britain's highest civilian award, for his amazing struggle to survive.

SUPERMAN TO THE RESCUE

Written by Janet Stewart
Illustrated by Rick Rowden

April in Phoenix, Arizona, is beautiful. For Debbie Williams and five others, Saturday, April 18, 1987, was a particularly special day. They were going to skydive from a plane, join hands, and drift slowly down to land in the desert below.

Anticipation filled the divers as they prepared to jump. Seconds into the jump, Debbie collided with Guy Fitzwater, a co-skydiver. Luckily, Guy was able to re-orient himself and pull the cord to open his parachute. But the collision had rendered Debbie unconscious and with terrifying speed, she plummeted like a 'rag doll' toward the desert.

Rescue for Debbie seemed an impossible feat! But, 25-year-old Gregory Robertson, an expert skydiver overseeing the jump in a freefall above them, wasn't discouraged. In a flash, he pinned his arms to his sides and brought his legs together, and dove head first toward Debbie. She had a head start though and was falling at an estimated speed of 240 kilometers an hour. Gregory would have to really fly to catch up!

Reaching where he thought Debbie would be, Gregory pulled up out of his dive. There she was - still ahead of him! Quickly, Gregory went into another dive. Reaching incredible speeds, he caught up with Debbie just as she entered the danger zone: If her parachute wasn't opened at this point, she would be doomed! Struggling to push Debbie into a sitting position, Gregory pulled the rip cord on her reserve parachute. Debbie was safe, but what about Gregory - he was entering a zone of no return! Then, pulling his own cord, his parachute opened and landed him safely in the desert.

THE EIGHTH DIVE

Written by Graham Roberts
Illustrated by Eugene Pawczuk

Seventeen-year-old Mark Smith borrowed his father's car and took his girlfriend, Nancy Burns, for a ride. After their outing on April 14, 1967, Mark decided he would wash the car at his father's marina. Pulling into the marina, he parked the red Mustang against a low curb that marked the edge of the seawall and the Miami River, two meters below.

After slipping the Mustang into first gear, Mark, concerned that Nancy would get dirty, suggested she remain in the car until he finished washing it. She agreed and tightly shut all the windows to prevent water from splashing inside.

Mark completed the task in about twenty minutes; all that remained for him to do was coil the hose and put it away. Nancy decided to listen to the radio and reached for the key, intending to turn it to the accessory mark. Being unfamiliar with the vehicle, she turned the switch too far - to ignition. The car immediately lurched forward over the curb, and for a moment its two front wheels hung in midair over the muddy water.

Dropping the hose, Mark sprang to the car, wrenching the driver's door open. The car swung to the right, smashing the door into a nearby river piling that immediately forced it shut, squeezing Mark out in the process. He threw himself across the car and managed to open the passenger door. The car was slowly tipping toward the river. Struggling to hold it back, he screamed at Nancy to "Get out!"

Nancy felt the car sway drunkenly above the water, but she dared not move or even breathe. Her body pressed hard into the seat, eyes wide in shocked surprise. The car rocked for a moment before pitching forward. It stood almost vertical, then plunged into the river, dragging Mark with it.

His ankle was trapped in the door and the car was above him. Mark had to free himself before it reached the riverbed or he would be trapped under it and drown. Miraculously, his foot came free after several hard kicks. Great bubbles of air accompanied Mark to the surface where, gasping for breath, he shouted "Nancy's still down there! Somebody has got to help her!" He gulped in a lung full of air and dove to Nancy's aid. Seconds passed as Mark searched through the dark, murky water; he couldn't even find the car. In despair, he surfaced, shaking from the effort. It was only the effort of several friends, concerned for his safety, that stopped him diving again.

Mark's father witnessed the accident and immediately called a local rescue unit. David Hurley, an Englishman, also saw the accident. He grabbed a coiled rope, tied one end to a piling, and dove into the river, taking the rope with him. In seconds he found the car lying on its side in five meters of water. He tried to open the door, but finally, after several tries, had to surface for air. The rescuers didn't know that the door they were trying to open had jammed after it smashed into the river piling. The other door was pressed into the mud.

Meanwhile, things happened so quickly, Nancy didn't have time to think until the car hit the water and began to sink. She watched in dread as water covered the windshield. Water quickly covered her legs, then swirled around her waist. Alone and frightened, a small voice told Nancy, "don't blow your cool!" It was her own. A recent Red Cross course at school had described survival techniques in water accidents. She tried to remember the rules: Stay calm, conserve oxygen, and look for air pockets; but where? Nancy looked around again, this time noticing there was less water in the back of the vehicle. She inched to the back of the car. It was too dark to see anything except billowing clouds of mud in the water above her. Small leaks caused the precious air pocket to slowly shrink.

Still calm, Nancy drifted into unconsciousness as the oxygen in the air bubble was used up.

Eight minutes passed before the rescue team arrived. They were able to reach the car, but every effort to open the door met with failure. Larry Norten, an experienced swimmer and life saver, dove to the car seven times over a ten-minute period. On his first dive he had been able to stay underwater for 60 seconds. Now, nearly exhausted, he could only manage fifteen-second dives before surfacing.

Nancy had been entombed nineteen minutes when Larry made his eighth dive. He counted off the seconds, conscious of his growing tiredness and pounding in his chest as he pushed himself to the limit. Two seconds to reach the car, he counted; thirteen left. He tapped on the window hoping for a response, even though he guessed she must be dead after being submerged for nearly twenty minutes. Something was different on this dive. On previous dives the car had been on its side and upright, but now it was half upright. Perhaps the river current had pushed it over? Larry swam to the bottom of the car where he found the door open just enough to get his hand inside. There was the danger that the car could roll back and trap him if he attempted to open the door further. If he thought about it, he did not let it deter him as he forced the door open. About twelve seconds had passed. In three or four seconds he would have to surface for air.

Suddenly, his hand touched a small sandaled foot. He grasped an ankle and gently pulled until his arm could encircle Nancy's waist and float her down into the front seat. Twenty seconds gone, he knew it would take much more time for him to wiggle back through the door with her. He was in desperate need of air. Then he felt Nancy's hand move, sending a shock of excitement and determination through him. She was still clinging to life! With a superhuman effort of will, Larry forced himself to continue the painfully slow process of guiding Nancy's body through the door. Once free of the car, Larry thrust Nancy to the surface, then followed himself.

Nancy was revived with oxygen. Her calm behavior and courage had helped in her quick recovery. Larry had remained underwater for 45 seconds, a remarkable feat of endurance, and one that Nancy will always remember.

SAVED BY A HAIR

Written by Bob Goodwin
Illustrated by Neil Humby

Have you ever heard the expression, "Saved by a hair?" Twenty-year-old Sherry Vyverberg of Rochester, New York, has. Sherry's life was saved by the hair on her head.

On May 30, 1983, Sherry, a nursing assistant, was visiting Niagara Falls, Canada. Niagara Falls is one of the Seven Wonders of the World. The Falls are divided into two parts: The Horseshoe Falls on the Canadian side of the Niagara River, and the American Falls on the U.S. side. It is estimated that over 7,000 cubic meters (245,000 cubic feet) of water pour over the two Falls every second of every day! It was into this cold, rough water that Sherry Vyverberg fell one early morning in May.

Sherry had been walking along an old concrete retaining wall near the power station, about 500 meters (1,600 feet) from the edge of the Horseshoe Falls. It was early in the morning with a warm sun climbing steadily overhead. Sherry and her two friends were excited about visiting the Falls to take in the spectacular scenery. The top of the old concrete wall was lined with slippery, wet moss, making the footing very dangerous. Sherry shouldn't have risked her life by walking along the top of the wall with the swift Niagara River flowing dangerously below. Sherry failed to see the danger. One minute she was perched on the moss-covered wall, the next she was in the freezing river.

Within seconds of falling off the wall, the swiftly flowing river sucked the young woman under, dragging her body toward the edge of doom. Sherry Vyverberg was not a good swimmer. For a moment, panic set in. Then she remembered her basic nurse's training - keep calm in any emergency. Rather than thrash and flail about in the fast-moving current, Sherry rolled onto her back and somehow managed to float to the surface. The current roared in her ears. Sherry knew that the Falls were only minutes away. Unless someone jumped in to save her, she was lost!

In fact, one of Sherry's friends, Gregory Grant, did jump into the water, right after Sherry fell in. But the cold water and the swiftly moving current were too much for him, forcing him back to shore. Another friend, Keith Gandy, ran toward the road bordering the river, yelling for help. Keith was hopping on one foot, his other locked in a cast from an earlier accident. Sherry was only minutes away from death!

Then Keith saw a truck. It was a utility truck owned by the Canadian Niagara Power Company, and there were three men inside. Keith hopped up and down, frantically waving his arms. The driver of the truck, John Marsh, an employee of the power company, stopped and got out. Keith hopped over and told Marsh what had happened. He pointed toward the wall where a soaking Gregory Grant stood shivering. Marsh was a volunteer firefighter as well as an expert scuba diver.

With his two workmates, Pete Quinlan and Joe Camissa, Marsh grabbed two lengths of rope from the back of the truck and ran to the river.

They saw Sherry bouncing in and out of the raging current. The three men ran along the riverbank, following the young woman's descent to the Falls. But, Sherry had drifted over 60 meters (200 feet) away from the shoreline. It seemed impossible!

John Marsh still wanted to try. He quickly tied the two lengths of rope together to form a single long strand. He wrapped one end around his waist and tied a tight knot. Camissa and Quinlan grabbed hold of the other end and braced themselves against the shoreline. It was now or never!

Taking a deep breath, John Marsh leapt away from the safety of the shoreline and dove into the swiftly flowing river. Instantly, the current grabbed at his body, dragging him toward the brink of the Falls. John relied on his scuba diving and swimming skills as he stroked bravely through the rough water. Several times he was submerged by the cascading river. Sharp, jagged rocks lining the river bottom tore at his arms and legs, but still he kept on! He looked up and saw Sherry, heading straight toward him.

But another danger loomed ahead. A concrete breakwater, built by the power company, jutted halfway out into the river. Sherry hit the breakwater and veered away from the brink of the Falls, heading instead toward the narrow sluice leading to the huge turbines of the power company. If she went through the turbines, her body would be crushed to death.

John Marsh had only one chance. With a mighty surge, he stroked furiously against the current, pulling to within a meter of the woman. Both Sherry and John were being dragged toward the deadly turbines. If the rope broke now, they were both doomed! But John wasn't thinking of that. He knew he could do it! With one last effort, John Marsh reached out against the force of the river and grabbed for the girl. He was in luck! He had grabbed Sherry by the hair - a whole handful of wet, blonde hair. He pulled Sherry toward him.

Camissa and Quinlan, watching anxiously from the shoreline, let out a cry of relief. They pulled hard on the rope against the dangerous current, dragging Sherry and John to safety. There wasn't a moment to lose. John had rescued Sherry less than 150 meters (500 feet) from the brink of the mighty Niagara Falls!